MW00745235

WORKS
of
HE*ART*

Compiled by Pat Cudimano

Published in the United States by

Great Quotations Publishing Inc.
1967 Quincy Court
Glendale Heights, IL 60139

Printed in Hong Kong
ISBN# 1-56245-038-7

For the artist in all of us.
May it flourish with
creative expression.

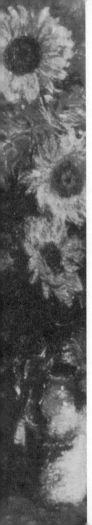

Art is called art because it is not nature.

Goethe

A good painter is to paint two main things, namely men and the working of men's mind.

Leonardo da Vinci

It's either easy or impossible.

Salvador Dali

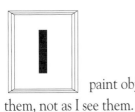 paint objects as I think them, not as I see them.

Pablo Picasso

A work of art has an author and yet, when it is perfect, it has something which is essentially anonymous about it.

Simone Weil

Art does not reproduce the visible; rather it makes it visible.

Paul Klee

5

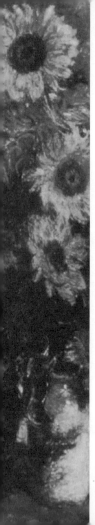

T hough we travel the world over to find the beautiful, we must carry it with us or we find it not.

Ralph Waldo Emerson

I dream my painting, and then I paint my dream.

Vincent van Gogh

Toulouse-Lautrec's distinctive lithographs introduced a unique style that helped shape the future of graphic art.

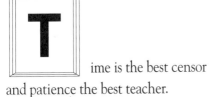 ime is the best censor and patience the best teacher.

Frederic Chopin

The artist, like the God of the creation, remains within or behind or beyond or above his handiwork, invisible, refined, out of existence, indifferent, paring his fingernails.

James Joyce

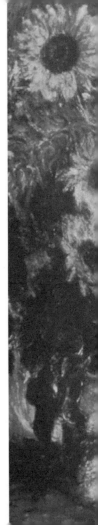

7

The imagination is certainly a faculty which we must develop, one which alone can lead us to the creation of a more exalting and consoling nature than the single brief glance at reality.

Vincent van Gogh

Art teaches nothing, except the significance of life.

Henry Miller

In art, as in love, instinct is enough.

Anatole France

A s a well-spent day
brings happy sleep, so life well used
brings happy death.

Leonardo da Vinci

Music is the language of spirits.
Its melody is like the frolicsome
breeze that makes the strings quiver
with love.

Kahlil Gibran

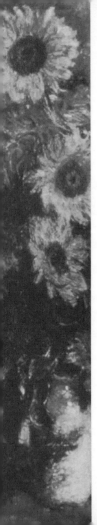

My art is the painting of the soul, so fine, so exacting, so strange: To blend in one tangible whole the manifold features of change.

Gamaliel Bradford

Everyone wants to understand painting. Why don't they try to understand the singing of birds? People love the night, a flower, everything that surrounds them without trying to understand them. But painting—that they *must* understand.

Pablo Picasso

Truth seems to come with its final word; and the final word gives birth to its next.

Rabindranath Tagore

In a letter to composer, Felix Mendelssohn, Goethe remarked, "I am Saul and you are David. Come to me when I am sad and discouraged and quiet my soul with your sweet harmonies."

Life imitates art far more than art imitates life.

Oscar Wilde

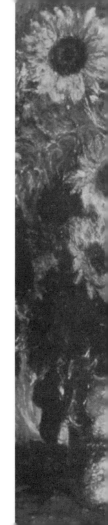

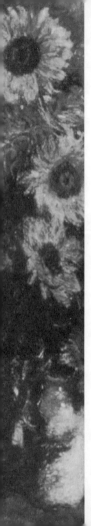

The more the marble wastes, the more the statue grows.

Michelangelo

It's as interesting and as difficult to say a thing well as to paint it. There is the art of lines and colors, but the art of words exists too, and will never be less important.

Vincent van Gogh

I do not seek. I find.

Pablo Picasso

The work of art must seize upon you, wrap you up in itself, carry you away. It is the means by which the artist conveys his passion; it is the current he puts forth which sweeps you along in his passion.

Pierre Auguste Renoir

All colors are the friends of their neighbors and the lovers of their opposites.

Marc Chagall

13

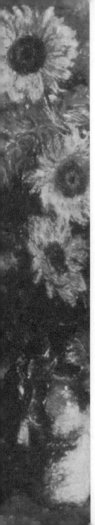

With our minds alone
we can discover those principles we
need to employ to convert all humanity
to success in a new, harmonious
relationship with the universe.

Buckminster Fuller

Everyone discusses [my art] and
pretends to understand, as if it were
necessary to understand when it is
simply necessary to love.

Claude Monet

Spanish cellist Pablo Casal's greatest love was conducting. While on his first American tour, he injured his fingers on his left hand. His initial response was, "Thank God I won't have to play the cello anymore."

Our doubts are traitors and make us lose the good we oft might win by fearing to attempt.

Shakespeare

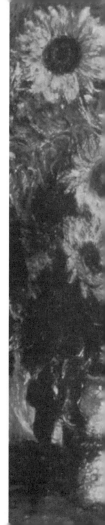

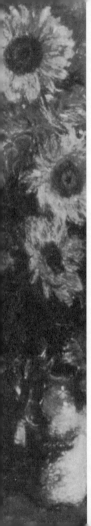

In reference to Mozart's immeasurable talent, Joseph Haydn once declared, "... nations would then vie with each other to possess so great a jewel within their frontiers."

Great Flemish painter, Sir Peter Paul Rubens, exhibited such keen intelligence and linguistic skills that he was often entrusted with important diplomatic missions. Charles I later knighted him for his service.

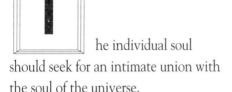

The individual soul should seek for an intimate union with the soul of the universe.

Novalis

Civilization is the lamb's skin in which barbarism masquerades.

Thomas Bailey Aldrich

Florentine painter, Sandro Botticelli, created a series of delicately intricate pen drawings which served as illustrations for Dante's Divine Comedy.

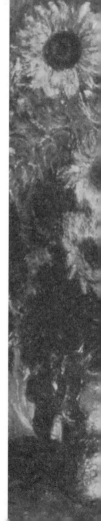

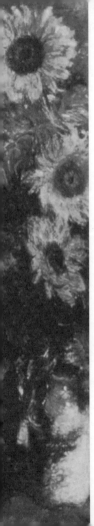

All artists bear the imprint of their time but the great artists are those in which this stamp is most deeply impressed.

Henri Matisse

Time ripens all things. No man's born wise.

Miguel de Cervantes

Every man has within himself a continent of undiscovered character. Happy is he who proves to be the Columbus of his spirit.

Johann Wolfgang von Goethe

The cello is like a beautiful woman who has not grown older, but younger with time, more slender, more supple, more graceful.

Pablo Casals

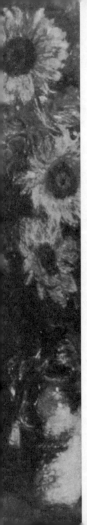

When broached on the subject of heaven and hell, French writer and artist, Jean Cocteau, declined to comment. He briefly explained, "I have friends in both places."

The composer of several memorable waltzes, Johann Strauss II, was never much of a dancer and avoided many a grand Viennese ball.

Experience has two things to teach: the first is that we must correct a great deal; the second, that we must not correct too much.

Delacroix

What is actual is actual only for one time and only for one place.

T.S. Eliot

If you ask me what I came to do in this world, I, an artist, will answer you: "I am here to live out loud."

Emile Zola

T here is nothing more difficult for a truly creative painter than to paint a rose, because before he can do so he has first to forget all the roses that were ever painted.

Henri Matisse

Happiness lies in the consciousness we have of it, and by no means in the way the future keeps its promises.

George Sand

Art is a lie that makes us realize truth.

Pablo Picasso

22

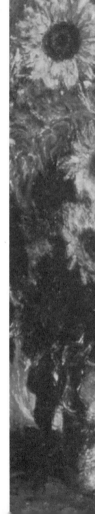

When one is a stranger to oneself then one is estranged from others too.

Anne Morrow Lindbergh

The key is what is within the artist. The artist can only paint what she or he is about.

Lee Krasner

In silence alone does a man's truth bind itself together and strike root.

Antoine de Saint-Exupery

23

How vain painting is—
we admire the realistic depiction of
objects which in their original state we
don't admire at all.

Blaise Pascal

Art, like life, should be free, since both
are experimental.

George Santayana

No bird soars too high, if he soars with
his own wings.

William Blake

Two roads diverged in a wood. I took the one less travelled by, and that has made all the difference.

Robert Frost

Articulate words are harsh clamor and dissonance. When man arrives at his highest perfection, he will again be dumb!

Nathaniel Hawthorne

25

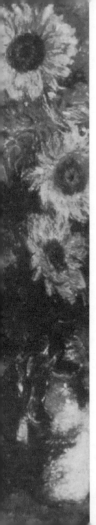

Pianist, Victor Borge, once explained to a friend that his piano keys were yellow not because of age but rather because "the elephant smoked too much."

Give me the luxuries of life and I will willingly do without the necessities.

Frank Lloyd Wright

Art plays an unknowing game with ultimate things, and yet achieves them!

Paul Klee

While I recognize the necessity for a basis of observed reality ... true art lies in a reality that is felt.

Odilon Redon

Traditions are lovely things - to create traditions, that is, not to live off them.

Franz Marc

The simple heart that freely asks in love, obtains.

John Greenleaf Whittier

27

Art distills sensation and embodies it with enhanced meaning in memorable form—or else it is not art.

Jacques Barzun

Our duty is to be useful, not according to our desires but according to our powers.

Henri Frederic Amiel

The object of art is to give life a shape.

Jean Anouilh

Without art, the crudeness of reality would make the world unbearable.

George Bernard Shaw

Painting is just another way of keeping a diary.

Pablo Picasso

Although in his later years Pierre Renoir was crippled with arthritis and had to have the brush strapped to his arm, he continued to create superb works of art.

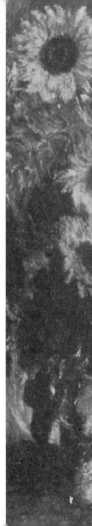

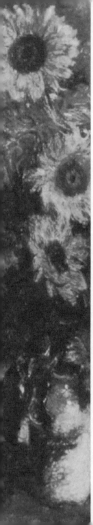

Only that day dawns to which we are awake.

Henry David Thoreau

Attracted by the mesmerizing Indian rhythms, Czech composer Antonin Dvorak combined native American music into his own compositions.

He alone knows what love is who loves without hope.

Friedrich von Schiller

A talent for drama is not a talent for writing, but is an ability to articulate human relationships.

Gore Vidal

In New York during 1961, Henri Matisse's painting "Le Bateau" had hung upside down in the Museum of Modern Art for 47 days before anyone noticed the mistake.

To a mind that is still, the whole universe surrenders.

Chuang-tse

31

If men of genius only knew what love their works inspire!

Hector Berlioz

He began a distinguished career in music at the age of three; he could play a composition after hearing it only once; he composed a prelude while writing a fuge—this was the creative genius of Wolfgang Amadeus Mozart!

There are divine things more beautiful than words can tell.

Walt Whitman

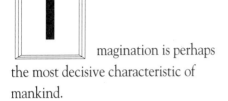 magination is perhaps the most decisive characteristic of mankind.

Max Beckmann

It is always self-defeating to pretend to the style of a generation younger than your own; it simply erases your own experience in history.

Renata Adler

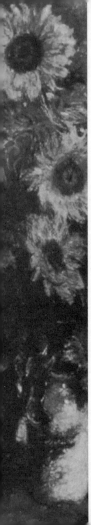

P oetry is the revelation of a feeling that the poet believes to be interior and personal [but] which the reader recognizes as his own.

Salvatore Quasimodo

French painter and sculptor, Edgar Degas, differed from his Impressionist colleagues in that he did not paint out of doors.

T he only means of strengthening one's intellect is to make up one's mind about nothing—to let the mind be a thoroughfare for all thoughts.

John Keats

Color, which is vibration just as music is, is able to attain what is most universal yet at the same time most elusive in nature: its inner force.

Paul Gauguin

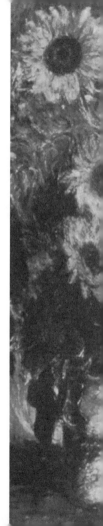

Upon his deathbed, French novelist, Honore de Balzac, is said to have requested that Dr. Bianchon be brought to his bedside. The good doctor however was a character from his novel *Le Comedie Humaine*.

Time is a fluid condition which has no existence except in the momentary avatars of individual people.

William Faulkner

Painter, sculptor, and architect, El Greco, always signed his work using his given name in Greek characters and often ending with "Kres" [Cretan].

Come forth, and bring with you a heart that watches and receives.

William Wordsworth

The strongest man on earth is he who stands most alone.

Henrik Ibsen

37

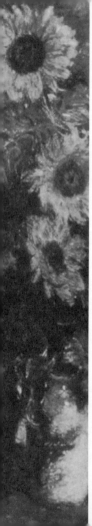

While on a stroll, Goethe and Beethoven had their conversation interrupted numerous times by admiring passersby. Noticing Goethe's increasing irritation, Beethoven remarked, "Do not let that trouble Your Excellency; perhaps the greetings are intended for me."

Composers should write tunes that chauffeurs and errand boys can whistle.

Sir Thomas Beecham

 rt is meant to disturb,
science reassures.

Georges Braque

It took almost a century to compile
and publish the complete works of
Johann Sebastian Bach—which
comprised 46 volumes.

An artist cannot speak about his art
any more than a plant can discuss
horticulture.

Jean Cocteau

A nation creates music —the composer only arranges it.

Mikhail Glinka

Before you contradict an old man, my friend, you should endeavor to understand him.

George Santayana

Experience is not what happens to you; it is what you do with what happens to you.

Aldous Huxley

A lexandre Dumas was such a prolific writer that he needed a team of ghostwriters to assist him. One day while speaking to his son who was also an exceptional writer, Dumas Sr. inquired, "Did you read my new novel yet?" His son responded, "No. Have you?"

When you're down and out, something always turns up—and it is usually the noses of your friends.

Orson Welles

Absences are a good influence in love and keep it bright and delicate.

Robert Louis Stevenson

When a newspaper mistakenly announced the death of Rudyard Kipling, the author immediately notified the editor with the message, "I've just read that I'm dead. Don't forget to delete me from your list of subscribers."

T o fall in love is to create a religion that has a fallible god.

Jorge Luis Borges

The awareness of our own strength makes us modest.

Paul Cezanne

When visiting a farm at the age of two, Mozart heard a pig squeal and proudly exclaimed, "G-sharp." Someone in the entourage found a piano and hit the key, verifying the young prodigy's claim.

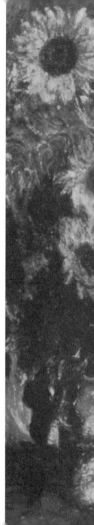

43

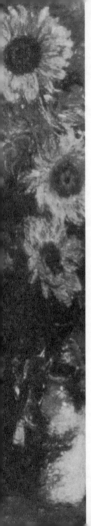

Is it not by love alone that we succeed in penetrating to the very essence of a being?

Igor Stravinsky

You need three things in the theatre— the play, the actors, and the audience, and each must give something.

Kenneth Haigh

The attitude that nature is chaotic and that the artist puts order into it is a very absurd point of view, I think. All that we can hope for is to put some order into ourselves.

Willem De Kooning

Our entire life, with our fine moral code and our precious freedom, consists ultimately in accepting ourselves the way we are.

Jean Anouilh

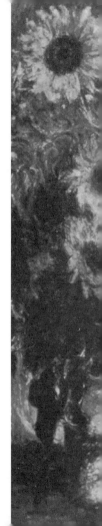

After a discouraging rehearsal in which several of the orchestra members were off in their timing, British conductor, Sir Thomas Beecham, singled out one of the culprits and asked, "We cannot expect you to be with us the whole time, but maybe you would be kind enough to keep in touch now and again?"

The moment you cheat for the sake of beauty, you know you're an artist.

Max Jacob

reat things are accomplished by men who are not conscious of the impotence of man. Such insensitiveness is precious.

Paul Valery

Life moves out of a red flare of dreams into a common light of common hours, until old age brings the red flare again.

William Butler Yeats

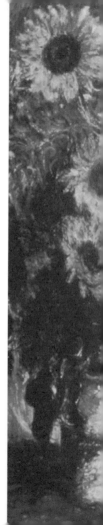

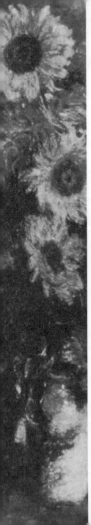

The toughest thing about success is that you've got to keep on being a success.

Irving Berlin

On one occasion, George Bernard Shaw and a friend were admiring a bust of Shaw that had been sculpted by Rodin, then Shaw casually remarked, "It's a funny thing about that bust. As time goes on it seems to get younger and younger."

 man is known by the company his mind keeps.

Thomas Bailey Aldrich

The answer to the last appeal of what is right lies within a man's own heart. Trust yourself.

Aristotle

Plenty of people wish to become devout, but no one wishes to be humble.

La Rochefoucauld

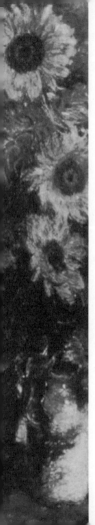

Loving-kindness is the better part of goodness. It lends grace to the sterner qualities of which this consists.

W. Somerset Maugham

At the age of six, conductor Gustav Mahler found a piano in his grandmother's attic and from that moment on his life was devoted to music.

A healthy adult male bore consumes each year one and a half times his own weight in other people's patience.

John Updike

Men reject their prophets and slay them, but they love their martyrs and honour those whom they have slain.

Fyodor Dostoyevsky

Oh Lord, it is not the sins I have committed that I regret, but those which I have had no opportunity to commit.

Ghalib

When asked why he did not frequent the movies, T.S. Eliot answered, "They interfere with my daydreams."

Now at last I have come to see what life is,

Nothing is ever ended, everything only begun,

And the brave victories that seem so splendid

Are never really won.

Sara Teasdale

Loving is half of believing.

Victor Hugo

The belief that becomes truth for me... is that which allows me the best use of my strength, the best means of putting my virtues into action.

Andre Gide

When a young musician began to criticize Brahms about publication postponements of his opus, Brahms retorted, "You can afford not to be immortal for a few more weeks."

The person who makes a success of living is the one who sees his goal steadily and aims for it unswervingly. That is dedication.

Cecil B. De Mille

It is indeed from the experience of beauty and happiness, from the occasional harmony between our nature and our environment, that we draw our conception of the divine life.

George Santayana

The world is a great volume, and man the index of that book; even in the body of man, you may turn to the whole world.

John Donne

On April 23, 1616 the world lost two of its most distinguished writers, William Shakespeare and Miguel de Cervantes.

One can pass on responsibility, but not the discretion that goes with it.

Benvenuto Cellini

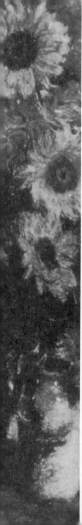

The notes I handle no better than many pianists. But the pauses between the notes - ah, that is where the art resides!

Artur Schnabel

One's outer life passes in a solitude haunted by the masks of others; one's inner life passes in a solitude hounded by the masks of oneself.

Eugene O'Neill

There are people who want to be everywhere at once and they seem to get nowhere.

Carl Sandburg

Reynolds said of Raphael: "It is from his having taken so many models that he became himself a model for all succeeding painters; always imitating and always original."

Inspiration could be called inhaling the memory of an act never experienced.

Ned Rorem

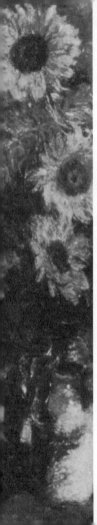

Human life is but a
series of footnotes to a vast, obscure,
unfinished masterpiece.

Vladimir Nabokov

Good actors are good because of the
things they can tell us without talking.
When they are talking, they are the
servants of the dramatist. It is what
they can show the audience when
they are not talking that reveals the
fine actor.

Cedric Hardwicke

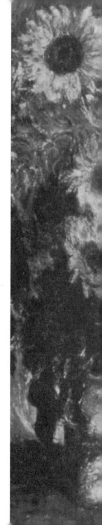

I n the long run men hit only what they aim at. Therefore, though they should fail immediately, they had better aim at something high.

Henry David Thoreau

When Edgar Degas' painting sold for an exorbitant sum at an auction, the artist compared the situation to how a horse must feel when the trophy is presented to the jockey.

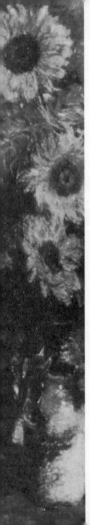

Half our life is spent trying to find something to do with the time we have rushed through life trying to save.

Will Rogers

All are but parts of one stupendous whole,

Whose body Nature is, and God the soul.

Alexander Pope

N atural abilities are
like natural plants, that need pruning
by study; and studies themselves do
give forth directions too much at large,
except they be bounded in by
experience.

Francis Bacon

After narrowly escaping injury during
the great San Francisco earthquake of
1906, Enrico Caruso promised never to
return to the city "where disorders like
that are permitted."

You cannot create genius. All you can do is nurture it.

Dame Ninette de Valois

No man is much pleased with a companion who does not increase, in some respect, his fondness of himself.

Samuel Johnson

I find my joy of living in the fierce and ruthless battles of life, and my pleasure comes from learning something.

August Strindberg

Is not this the true romantic feeling—not to desire to escape from life, but to prevent life from escaping you?

Thomas Wolfe

French Impressionist painter, Camille Pissarro, helped younger artists like Gauguin and Cezanne and also served as a peacemaker among this revolutionary group.

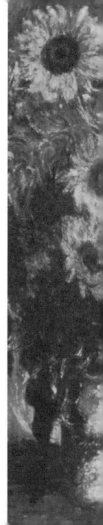

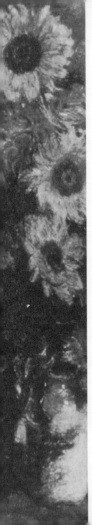

F or one human being to love another; that is perhaps the most difficult of all our tasks, the ultimate, the last test and proof, the work for which all other work is but preparation.

Rainer Maria Rilke

The important thing is to pull yourself up by your own hair to turn yourself inside out and see the whole world with fresh eyes.

Peter Weiss